BUGS

BEES AND WASPS

By William Anthony

KidHaven PUBLISHING

Published in 2022 by
KidHaven Publishing, an Imprint of Greenhaven Publishing, LLC
353 3rd Avenue
Suite 255
New York, NY 10010

Edited by: John Wood
Designed by: Amy Li

Find us on

Cataloging-in-Publication Data

Names: Anthony, William.
Title: Bees and wasps / William Anthony.
Description: New York : KidHaven Publishing, 2022. | Series: Bugs | Includes glossary and index.
Identifiers: ISBN 9781534537545 (pbk.) | ISBN 9781534537569 (library bound) | ISBN 9781534537552 (6 pack) | ISBN 9781534537576 (ebook)
Subjects: LCSH: Bees--Juvenile literature. | Wasps--Juvenile literature.
Classification: LCC QL565.2 W555 2022 | DDC 595.79'9--dc23

Printed in the United States of America

CPSIA compliance information: Batch #CSKH22: For further information contact Greenhaven Publishing LLC, New York, New York at 1-844-317-7404.

Please visit our website, www.greenhavenpublishing.com. For a free color catalog of all our high-quality books, call toll free 1-844-317-7404 or fax 1-844-317-7405.

PHOTO CREDITS – Images are courtesy of Shutterstock.com. With thanks to Getty Images, Thinkstock Photo and iStockphoto.
Cover – blackzheep, Karramba Production, Ermak Oksana, ten43, Africa Studio, In Art, azure1, LanKS, irin-k, Kletr, aodaodaodaod. Recurring Images – ten43, THPStock (paper), Africa Studio (header texture), kavram (main background), In Art, Kozyreva Elena (vector bees in header), Karramba Productions (parchment), Andrey Eremin, Steve Paint (labels), azure1 (magnifying glass), Ortis, LanKS, Popatov Alexander (page decoration), Ermak Oksana (doodles). P1 – blackzheep, irin-k, p2-3 – ER_09, p4-5 – Frederico Rostagno, KETPACHARA YOOSUK, p6-7 – Kovtun Petro, Nicola Dal Zotto, p8-9 – Craig Taylor, Mirko Graul, p10-11 – Krasowit, MRS.NUCH SRIBUANOY, le pur photography, p12-13 – Lehrer, p14-15 – Jack Hong, azur13, Subbotina Anna p16-17 – kosolovskyy, Lehrer, weter78, p18-19 – Jens Heidler, pixelnest, p20-21 – Computer Earth, Irina Kozorog, rtbilder, p22-23 – Gelpi, StockSmartStart, Chaikom, Mike McDonald, p24 – blackzheep.

CONTENTS

Words that look like **THIS** can be found in the glossary on page 24.

EXPLORER TRAINING

Hi there! Do you think you could help us out? We're a team of explorers and we need a new member. However, first we need to train you.

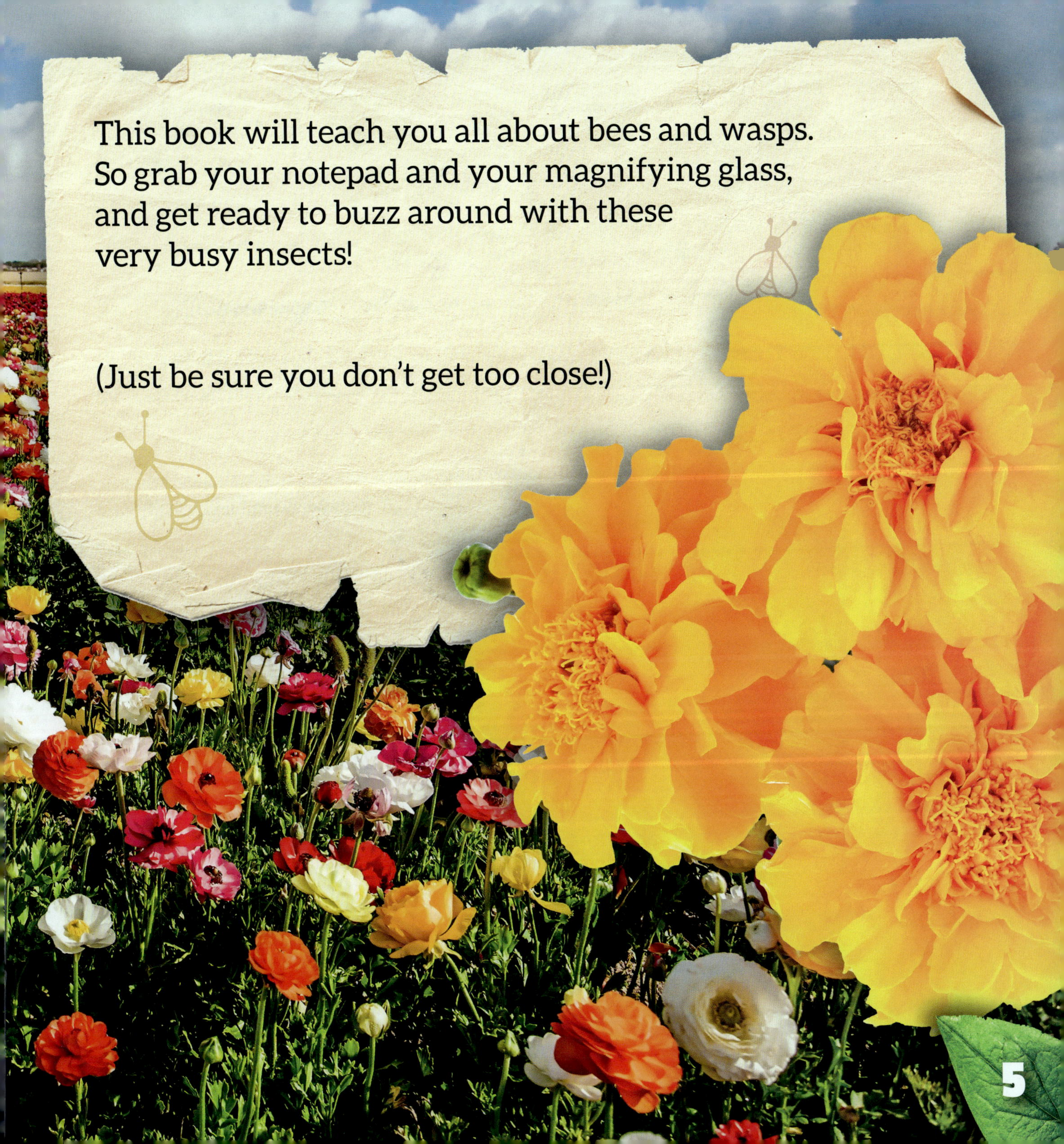

This book will teach you all about bees and wasps. So grab your notepad and your magnifying glass, and get ready to buzz around with these very busy insects!

(Just be sure you don't get too close!)

WHAT ARE BEES AND WASPS?

To start off, we need to know about each part of a bee and a wasp. They're both insects. Insects have no backbones and have six legs attached to their bodies.

Both animals have two pairs of buzzing wings to help them fly, and two antennae to help them **SENSE** the world around them. However, most bees and wasps are best known for their yellow and black patterns.

ADAPTATIONS

Like other bugs, bees and wasps have **ADAPTED** over time to have lots of special **FEATURES**. Female bees and wasps both have a stinger at the bottom of their abdomens.

Both insects use their stinger to attack things that they think might hurt them or their nest. They can also alert others in their **COLONY** to attack at the same time.

HOME LIFE

Bees and wasps live in different types of homes. Honeybees live in a **HIVE**, where they work as a team to raise young bees and make honey. However, most bees don't live in hives.

Some bees live in underground nests, such as this bumblebee nest.

All types of wasps live in nests. They make their nests by chewing up wood **FIBERS** and using the sticky mixture to build a home. Look – there's a potter wasp building its nest!

MEET THE COLONY

Many bees live on their own, but some bees live in colonies. Honeybees are colony bees, and they all work together. In each colony there are workers, drones, and a queen.

Each colony has one queen, who gives birth to other bees. Drones are males, and they **MATE** with the queen. Worker bees are female, and they gather food and look after young bees.

HIVE MIND

Honeybees work together to keep their hive running well. Each bee knows its job in the team. One of the most important jobs is collecting nectar and pollen.

Nectar and pollen are found in plants.

Worker bees leave the hive to collect nectar and pollen from different plants. Nectar is a sugary **LIQUID** and pollen is like powder. Honeybees collect them both for a very important reason – food.

FINDING A FEAST

Pollen is mixed with nectar to make bee bread. This is used to feed many of the young bees while they grow up. Adult bees eat honey.

Honey is made from nectar. Nectar has water in it, so the bees pass it to each other using their mouths until most of the water is gone. It turns into honey, and it is stored in the hive.

Wasp eating a strawberry

Wasps don't eat the same food as bees. They are omnivores, which means they eat both plants and other animals. Most wasps will eat a mixture of plants, nectar, and other insects.

Have you ever found lots of wasps gathering around your food at a picnic? Some wasps, such as yellow jacket wasps, will feed on human food if they can find it.

This wasp is enjoying some jam.

KOOKY BEES AND WACKY WASPS

Bees and wasps make a buzzing sound when they fly. That's the sound of their four wings flapping around 200 times in one second. That's so fast that we can't see each flap!

You might know a lot about bees, but did you know that they have some awesome dance moves? Honeybees perform a "waggle dance" to let others know where to find food.

The honeybee shakes its abdomen in the shape of an eight very quickly.

TIME TO EXPLORE

Well, that's the end of your training. Good news – you've passed! You are now ready to go out and explore the wilderness, armed with your new knowledge. But there's one more thing you'll need before you go...

…your well-earned explorer's badge! Here it is, and it means you are now a bee and wasp expert. Why not make your own badge and wear it with pride? Well done, explorer!

GLOSSARY

adapt to change over time to suit the environment

colony a group of animals living in one place

feature an interesting or important part

fiber something that is like a thread

hive a structure where bees live; a hive can be man-made or natural

liquid a material that flows, such as water

mate to produce young with an animal of the same species

sense to feel or be aware of

venom a harmful substance that is injected through a bite or a sting

INDEX